Chanukah

COLORING BOOK

FREDDIE LEVIN

DOVER PUBLICATIONS, INC.
MINEOLA, NEW YORK

NOTE

Chanukah is a happy holiday. Jews around the world remember how Judah Maccabee and his brothers fought many years ago to take back their temple for their people. There was only a bit of oil for the temple light, but this tiny bit lasted for eight days! That's why Jews light one candle for each night, using the menorah. There are special foods to eat, such as latkes (potato pancakes), and games to play, such as spinning the dreidel—a top with Hebrew letters on its sides. Have fun coloring the pictures in this book, which will tell you all about Chanukah!

Copyright

Copyright © 2011 by Dover Publications, Inc.
All rights reserved.

Bibliographical Note

Chanukah Coloring Book is a new work, first published by Dover Publications, Inc., in 2011.

International Standard Book Number
ISBN-13: 978-0-486-48286-6
ISBN-10: 0-486-48286-3

Manufactured in the United States by Courier Corporation
48286301
www.doverpublications.com

It's almost time for Chanukah!

There's lots to do to get ready.
Hannah polishes the menorah.

Hannah and Noah are making decorations.

4

Sasha is having fun, too.

Dad reads the story of Judah Maccabee.

On the first night, there is one candle to
light, plus the Shamash.

Mom lights the first candle and they all
sing the blessing.

Hannah stirs the batter to make latkes.

Dad fries the latkes.

It's the second night of Chanukah.

Latkes for supper. YUM!

Hannah, Noah and Mom dance the Hora.

On the fourth night of Chanukah, the family uses the menorah Noah made in pre-school.

On the fifth night of Chanukah, they use the
menorah Hannah made in Sunday school.

Grandma and Grandpa come to visit.

Grandma and Grandpa brought Chanukah
gifts for Hannah and Noah.

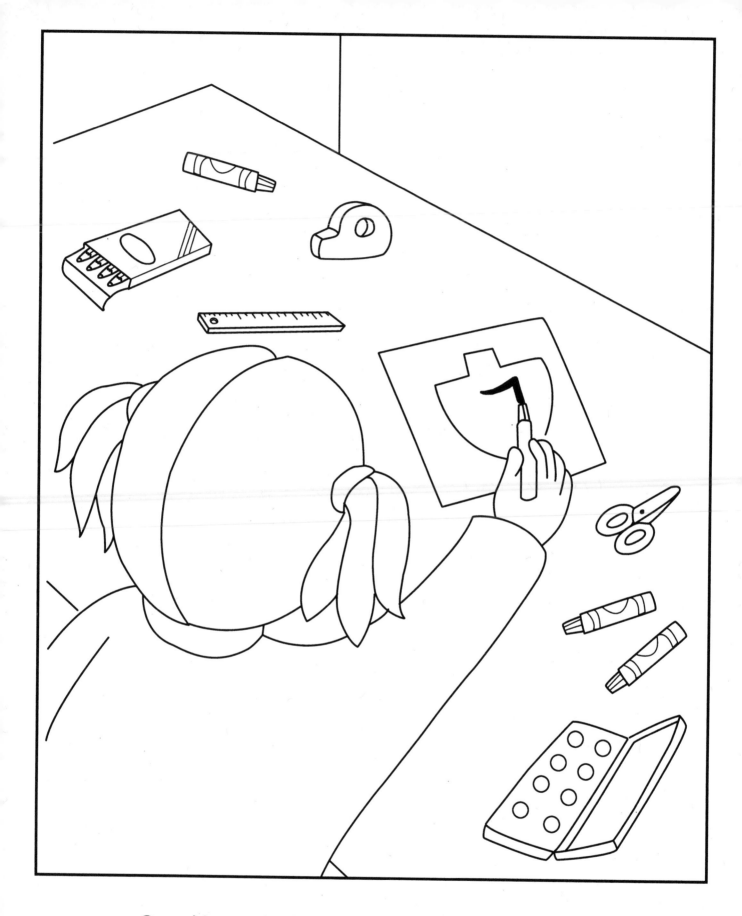

On the sixth night of Chanukah,
Hannah makes more decorations.

Noah pretends he is Judah Maccabee.

On the seventh night of Chanukah,
Hannah and Noah play Dreidel.

On the eighth night of Chanukah,
all the candles are lit.

Everything gets put away for next year.

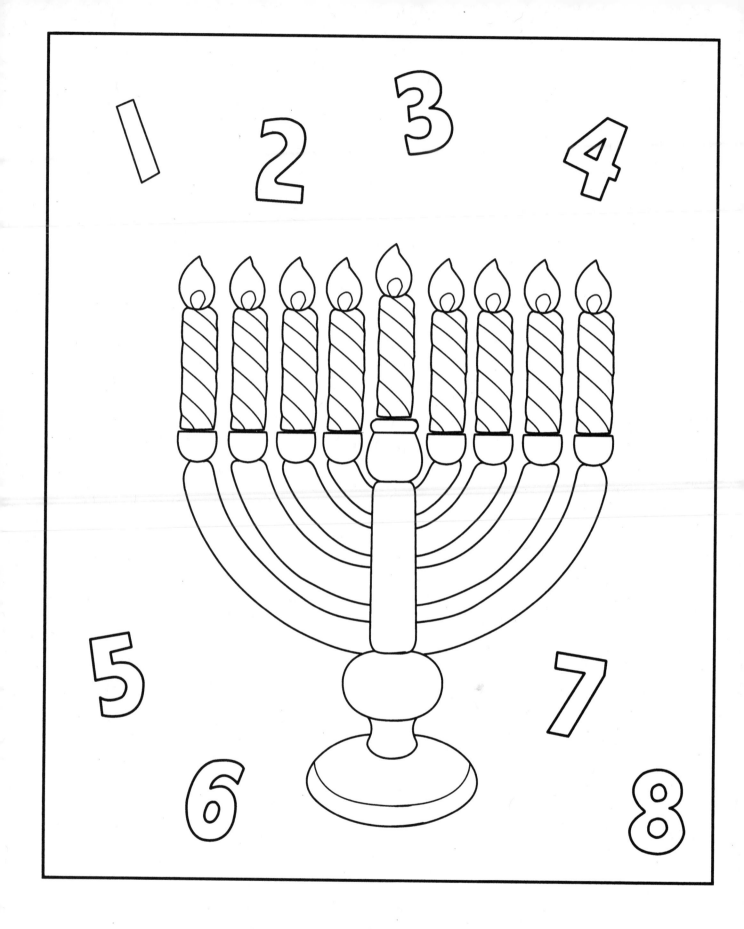

Eight nights of Chanukah!